Growing Pains

Victoria Kimbrell

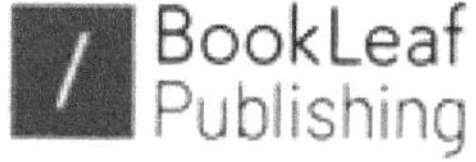

BookLeaf Publishing

Presentation by *BookLeaf Publishing*

Web: www.bookleafpub.com

E-mail: info@bookleafpub.com

ISBN: 9789357211413

First edition 2022

My Head is Filled With Poetry

When the sun and moon kissed each other in the
secrecy of time,
I wonder if they planned on my existence all these
years later,
or if I was a surprise that rose from the grit of the
ground,
out from between my mothers legs like a flower
blooming full.

I am an accumulation of brisk morning walks,
and senseless giggles in the quiet of a living room.
I don't know how to dance gracefully and never
learned to sing,
but I know how to spin and scream and laugh and
laugh.

So when the waves and winds hugged each other in
the quiet of storms,
I wonder if they expected a force like me to walk
their earth.
Did they know my feet would pound the sands into
the ground,
kick up shells and scream at the sea for the things I
can't change?

I'm a collection of busy fingers and clumsy hands,
chipped nails and crooked grins with clear intentions.

I wait for the chance to chase dreams that taunt me,
never knowing how to stay still or quiet and never
understanding why I'd need to.

For when the old stars and new soils slipped into each
other to craft me,
they built me from my soles up of speckled skin and
spindly hair.
They made my squared shoulders and filled my head
with poetry,
gave me an aching back to carry me and all my
memories through a lifetime.

So why would I strive to alter the creation
the entire universe worked so hard to fabricate?
Why would I ever wish to silence the being
the entire cosmos worked so delicately to design?

Droplet Kisses

I smelled the first rain today,
and it reminded me of monkey bars and swing sets.
Trampolines in backyards and bandaids on bruises,
the way you'd pinky promise to love me always,
and I'd pinky swear to tell the truth.

My legs ran fast when I was small, feet hit the asphalt
like slaps.
I didn't ever turn my head to look at who was behind
me,
nor check the ground for bumps or cracks.
There was a plastic pool for every hot day,
and a lullaby with the stroke of my nose for each
restless night.

So when I heard the first droplets kiss the ground
today,
it reminded me of that age.
The one where everything counted but nothing
mattered,
where I could break my bones and they'd grow back
stronger,
ready to play tag ferociously through woodchips and
barkdust.

The time when grass was made to roll in,
bubbles blown just to pop,

science experiments the epitome of magic in my
mind
When the earth was only 4 feet away from my point
of view,
and people all seemed big and in control.

So as I watched the water slap the street,
like my feet used to hit the pavement,
I couldn't help but have envy for those days.
The blissfulness of barbies,
and the ease of sugary serotonin filled evenings.

You don't get candy for your cuts after 10.
There isn't school lunches with love notes,
or roller rinks with light up wheels.
Certainly nobody to curl into when a scrape slices
you,
nor to blot your tears with the pads of their thumbs.

But there is the first rain,
the smell of new beginnings,
the fresh wash of the earth,
the sigh that follows inhaling fresh soil scents,
and the weight the drops seem to always rinse away.

Most Days

Most days are filled with airy thoughts.
They don't keep the ground from creaking under my steps,
or the door from unlatching with my eager hands.
I wake up in yellow and am bathed in bed with blue.
The sun echoes on the walls and a parched tickle
urges me up.
I hum to the kitchen and swallow berries and eggs,
bask in the sun and lounge in the living room,
find a friend to go distract ourselves from existing,
fall asleep with stars behind my lids and do it again.

Some days though I wake up wrong.
Jolt myself out of the reality I am used to,
but wallow in dirty sheets nonetheless.
My bones quite literally cease to stand the weight of
me.
I forget the names of all my friends,
convince myself my memories are false,
no good things have ever happened,
and all those most days disappear.

Those some days scare me when they stretch on end,
when January turns to February and I haven't seen
myself in weeks,
looked in the mirror but couldn't look at myself right,
because I'm quite unsure of who I actually want to
be.

I sit there and crave simple affection and care,
and convince myself I have none, from others or my
own brain,
empty my tears on the shower wall instead of going
to sleep,
and let the water hug me while I watch it circle the
drain.

Then I'll wake up one morning in yellow golden
warmth.
I'll carry on like it was just a month long bad dream,
like I haven't lost a minute nor second of time.
I'll pick the clothes off my floor and wash my face in
the sink,
shower and scrub the film of stagnancy off my skin,
wonder when things got so messy all the sudden.
No bricks in my brain, just airy thoughts and peace of
mind,
stars behind my lids and hope for the most days to
last longer this time.

Highway 20

I bet the dents in the carpet of the floor I used to call
home are gone
from my tired back laying beside the fireplace while
having conversation,
and I am almost sure the clock doesn't tick the same;
It moves much faster.

My sister's hair grows each time I visit, my brother
stands taller each month.
The language of siblings I once understood seems to
be lost to my brain,
foreign jokes I have no part of told and retold without
my presence to giggle along.

A long road separating us is so much more than a
bedroom wall,
through a screen never seems to hold the same,
and I feel the absence of their youthfulness.

It is hard growing up and growing away,
losing the connection of silly antics and shared
boredom,
seeing your mother age and your family live a life
that doesn't involve you.

Everyone just keeps growing, turning new stones and
gaining new memories,

And I never have the time to slow down, nobody ever
has the time to slow down.
Everyone is aging faster than I can drive the highway
back home.

And it hurts.

My Mother's Embrace

How do I crawl into my mother's lap at 21,
make her hold all 150 pounds of my weight?
Because I want the warmth of a body that will love
me as I am,
the safety of arms that have no ill intentions.

Do I call her on the phone to tell her I am on my way,
or just show up on her doorstep unannounced?
Will her soft touch heal my aches and pains,
or do I have to do that by myself?

Her way of Caring

The universe has been playing games with me.
First birthing me to a family that could never love me
right,
and raising me with a father who was far too harsh
with words.

She then opened me to boys who didn't care,
and let me think I didn't matter for years on end,
taking people that helped build my foundation,
plucking them from my life and making me watch
them leave.

She challenged me with problems I still can't quite
yet solve,
and hurdles that all 5 feet 5 inches of me can't scale
to this day.
I spent a lot of time cursing her name this past year.

I screamed and kicked every time clouds approached
my horizon,
because I finally understood what I deserved and she
still wasn't letting me have it.

I'm now learning to bathe myself in her rain,
taking the storms she throws my direction, and
finding rhythm to dance in them.
I think she tricked me all those times so I could enjoy
the sunny patches more.

Because even through all her games, the universe has
also sent me gifts,
people I've made homes out of and friends that
taught me how to laugh,
places that I'd never dream of and scenery made of
flowers and fields,
She gave me this body, this mind, the words that spill
from my fingertips to paper.

I think she cares for me in a way that demands
gratitude and encourages growth.
I think her love doesn't fade with the sun,
I think it grows through the storms.

I think she knows exactly what's best for me,
and the exact amount of rain I can bare upon my
shoulders.

Words Between Sisters

I stared at your estranged face across the table and
realized how similar we were.
Cut from the same cloth and made into different
quilts,
how could I forget we were crafted together.

You say you are afraid to stand up for yourself, and I
am too.
I say I didn't know how to stay, and you say you
understand why I left.
We skate around the intimacy of each other's
company,
sipping tea when the chatter goes silent.

We are getting better, healing from this gaping
childhood between us.
What would he think of us, sitting here proclaiming
self discovery,
navigating relationships and finding a life of our own.

You know we have all the power,
for his name will perish in our mouths,
turn bitter and rot in our skulls once they are put in
the ground,
and nobody will ever speak it again.

Trade Street Memories

It is hard to hate the person who spun fairy tales to
fall asleep to.

You'd carried the weight of me by piggyback,
through haunted houses and corn fields too.
You'd grasp my fingers so tightly round the roller
rink,
give smiles of encouragement when my confidence
grew.

It's impossible to forget the bliss in those Trade Street
memories.

Turtle shells, lizard tails, and a dog who I no longer
knew,
playing board games to pass time on those dirty
wooden floors,
singing songs in pj bottoms and sliding in socks with
no use for shoes,
the crunching of autumn leaves as we run down to the
creek.

I still hum around the house and have aches for the
color blue.

I collect things with intent and am fascinated by the
ocean's depth,

I crave the architecture of a Victorian home with a
porch swing and sun room.
I look for ways to have my soles in dirt, never
forgoing my love for bleu cheese,
and when I see myself in the light of a mirror it's easy
to pick out pieces of you.

I suppose that is why it hurts so bad to convince
myself your existence is minute.

To pretend you don't live in my mind,
every April 9th and September 2,
October 19th, December 25th,
and any other day I'm reminded of you.

At this point it is my hope you've forgotten.

For every car ride to me and each 30 minute
commute,
I pray to my cream ceilings I am erased from your
thoughts,
that you don't mutter "I love you forever" to an
empty abandoned room,
and your radio never plays the songs we used to sing.

I can't fathom causing that pain, certainly not
something I would choose.

Did you know your number in my phone has never
been removed?
Just in case, on the chance, if I ever feel the need,

If I ever want to destroy all this time I've put between
us two,
I'll give you a call and watch my world burn.

I hope I never come to that, but I do think about it
through and through.

Enough For You

I am thin as ice,
cracked from the pressures of others,
bare and cold and stiff.

I will take the shreds of cloth on my back
and place them onto your smoothed shoulders,
shiver in the dead of night,
to keep you comfortable on a summer eve.

What wrong can you commit that I won't forgive?
I will always forget your flaws and faithless words.
What harm could you do that I won't fix?
I will always bend to mend the breaks in your spine,

stitch up all your open wounds,
lick the salt off your palms,
ice your bruised knees with frozen berries,
and clear the ground of which you walk.

I'll crawl into bed with my skin and bones,
gray hollowed eyes and sunken in cheeks,
all bare and cold and stiff,
and a smile will still be brazen on my lips.

Because these bones cared and this skin gave.
Because when I am left with nothing, you will hold
everything I had to give,
and only everything I had will be enough for you to
take.

I See Her

I spotted her on the stone paths of a college not far
from home,
and on the linoleum of the kitchen floor in the
morning,
dancing round and round to music
nobody else can hear.

She's louder than noise itself and I remind her,
"shh quiet down and listen"
only for her to jump in circles with energy she begs
to share
with anybody who's willing to receive.

Sometimes I see her on the shores off the Pacific,
running from the waves and giggling in a frenzy.
Other times she's tucked in the forest under a blanket
of trees,
thoughts spinning slowly above her head
as bees buzz around her skull.

Tonight I listened to her cry in the warmth of a lamp,
through the walls of a room filled with colors of
green and splashed with art,
so lately I've been spending more time with her,
letting her know I love her just as much as anyone
else, even more so.

I found her, I see her, I hear her,

and I will always be in her bones,
giving her the love she desires to have,
the love she needs to grow and thrive.

I Look For It

I used to think love was weak,
hid it away underneath a shelf of books,
where nobody ever looks,
stuffed it underneath cold sheets and heavy blankets,
hushed and smothered with indifference.

But now that I know that love is strength,
I look for it each place I go,
finding it in the reflections of puddles,
how they make the world seem still and peaceful,
in the pines of trees, sharp and cunning with grit.

I embrace love so much that sometimes I think I see
it
when there isn't really any there to be found at all;
on your pillowcase, so warm on my face,
the freckles smiling at me across your nose, fingers in
my hair.
I get the words affection and attention mixed in my
head.

But I couldn't know the difference,
because I give love so quickly,
flooding with minutes in my day made for you,
words I've only let you see,
and caresses I'd never give others unless they asked.

My life is more colorful this way though, with love in
it.
Even when the love leaves,
and when it's taken from my chest,
even when it was never there to begin,
and I was a fool the whole time though,

I'd never had the same joy before I had those lovely
hues.
So I chase the colors like wind chases stray hair,
and run from the grays that used to consume me,
finding strength in each splashed puddle and fallen
pine,
finding love in every single one of my days.

In the letters of old book shelves,
in the comfort of soft sheets,
in the hushed whisper of a secret language;
I look for it,
even if there isn't really any there to be found at all.

Unconditionally Sweet

21

He never searches for more than I am willing to give.

In the shower when he hugged me,
slid his lips over mine just to kiss me,
so full of kindness, tenderness never fleeting.

He said in the car on the way to meet my family,
he'd wish for nothing more than to just be around me.
He touches me like I deserve to be handled with the
care of an age old art piece,
and he never wants to take any more of me than I
already offer for him to receive.

The only one who has ever made me feel complete,
and because of him I finally know what loving
someone means,
to be patient and kind, and unconditionally sweet.

Home

I enjoyed imagining making a home out of him.

Being welcomed by his arms every evening under our
shared roof,
and waking up to him as the sun bathed us together.

My brain made up scenarios.

Breakfast with shared jokes we only held between us,
Night times where I tired first so he held me until I
slept.

I dreamt of a settled life filled with slow mornings.

A shared experience though the ebbs and flows of
life,
where ease took the form of a person, happiness a
shared presence.

A reality of long term love, and it was beautiful.

My Dollhouse

They look through my window to see the woman
who lives in the glow of a lamp, and they walk by my
dollhouse drawing their perceptions of who I am.

She kisses ones who steal her heart away in the night,
and lift her to the ceiling.
She reads books and studies the screen in front of her,
with intensity and furrowed brows.

She burns incense and waters her plants each week,
humming along to old music her mother was raised
on.
She dances in the mornings when the sun rises,
and spins records in the corner to feel free.

They look through my window to see the woman I've
always wanted to be,
and they walk by my dollhouse peering into panes
I've painted for them to admire.

A Lovers Embrace

24

The small of my back was made for your tummy to
rest against,
just as the shallows of your collarbone were meant to
hold my head,
as if the universe made our bodies to fit together.

Not like puzzle pieces that snap into place,
just people who were bound by some cheesy cosmic
destiny
to hold each other the way they had never held
another before.

The Weight of Loss

Loss is a consuming emotion you wake up dizzy
from.
Debilitated, dehydrated and stiff, heavy in places that
used to feel light.

Loss is also paired with relief, a sensation whose
close acquaintance is peace,
"I'm glad it's over, this is the worst of it, move on,
move on, move on."

In the wake of loss emerges kindred souls,
the people who are there after the fall and take you in
with warm embraces.

These are the people who throw open their arms,
welcome your sadness as theirs,
taking the weight of loss and spreading it across their
own scarred shoulders.

Gentle smiles and soft words to combat the chaos of
echoing thoughts;
these are the ones who hold the recipe for comfort
cooked to perfection.

So the words I write today aren't for the reading of
those who've brought this loss,
but for the hearts of the people who've held me
steady from the start.

Time Heals All

I'm letting time work on me.
Letting the dust settle in my bones,
while my memories are swept away
by months of living and forgetting.

Tick tock
I forget the way your tongue presses your teeth when
you smile.
I forget how you rub my thumb with yours while our
fingers are laced.

Tick tock
The sight of you working your way up slowly to kiss
me softly is gone.
The touch of your sweet lips on my neck while you
hold me no longer exists.

I am letting time work on me.
Listening to the blood flow in my ears,
so the silk of your voice can be left behind
day by day, hour by hour.

Tick tock
You cannot miss something you do not recall,
and I cannot fathom missing you forever.

Beautiful Places

Sometimes I find myself in beautiful places,
Queen Anne's lace in my peripheral,
blue canvas and cotton clouds in focus,
your voice bouncing off the branches.

I sink into the earth like a grave,
feel the ground make room for my body,
welcoming me in with warm soils,
soothing me with soft winds.

Lights flicker in the distance,
cars seem to be ants and houses specks,
coupled with falling leaves and broken branches,
none of it is of any importance.

The stars begin to speckle the sky,
and I let my thoughts roam free.
I don't know why we live in boxes,
when crystals fill our air each night.

I try to fathom how to be happy when I come down,
to let go of the lazy buzz from my unoccupied hilltop,
but I'm hooked on the feel of the breeze on my face,
an addict for all the swaying grasses in sight.

I find myself yearning for the next time,
the next day I can lay in the bed of Her field,
the next evening I can let the earth hug me,

Her embrace is the most accepting I've ever known.

She nourishes those who burn her,
gives air to the ones who squeeze Her lungs,
tightly, tightly with their cold metal hands.
She still pulls the sun up to their horizon everyday.

Maybe I idolize Her,
seeing the resilience of Her oceans,
the forgiveness in Her forests,
mirroring Her selflessness and making it my own.

How I want Her grace,
how I admire Her beauty.
I only wish to stay here forever,
I only yearn to be more like Her.

Blooming With Tulips

29

I am opening myself once again to the world.
Throwing my head back with arms out to soak in the
spring sky,
whether the clouds have cover or the sun shines.

I am cradling the same shadows I've looked at in fear,
nursing them and accepting them like they are kin.

I want to encourage my body to change with the
seasons,
and this is the time for growth and new beginnings.

I want to bloom with the tulips and flourish with the
daffodils,
and with the sun I want to rise, more full and
complete than ever before,
more growth to look forward to than the horizon
itself.

Centered

I am the one that my sun orbits,
and the one from which my moon draws gravity.
I stand, more connected to the earth than I've ever
been,
and because of that, more free than I've ever felt.

How dare I ever feel guilty
for being at the middle of my own universe.

In my own body,
in my own home,
with my own people,
at the center of my own world.

How dare I ever feel selfish
for putting myself here and enjoying it.

I Still Hold Her

When I laid my head down on the pillow,
I felt my ten year old self tap on my shoulder
and whisper in my ear how proud she was.
I felt her hand hold mine because I was tangible proof
she had made it.

I felt her tears dampen the comforter
because she was so happy it wouldn't last forever,
and when it was over she could see
just how bright it was years down the line.

She could feel my heart beat faster than it ever had
before,
see my thoughts work harder than they ever had
before.
She could hear me laughing louder than I ever had
before,
see my feet dancing more freely than they ever had
before.

She looked at me with hope and I looked at her with
nostalgia.
We drifted to sleep and cradled our favorite parts of
each other
that would never get to meet,
but would always be a part of us.

www.ingramcontent.com/pod-product-compliance
Lightning Source LLC
LaVergne TN
LVHW021340200726